READ ABOUT

Out in Space

Robin Kerrod

WARWICK PRESS
New York/London/Toronto/Sydney

Published in 1989 by Warwick Press,
387 Park Avenue South, New York, New York 10016.
First published in 1989 by Kingfisher Books Ltd.
Copyright © Grisewood & Dempsey Ltd. 1989.

Library of Congress Catalog Card No. 88-51434
ISBN 0-531-19053-6

Printed in Spain

Contents

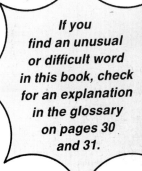

If you find an unusual or difficult word in this book, check for an explanation in the glossary on pages 30 and 31.

Lift-off!

The last few seconds of the countdown are ticking away. Check seat belts. Check instruments. Check communications. Five, four, three, two, one, zero!

You hear the roar and feel the thump as the rockets fire beneath you. You are on your way, starting another journey into space. In less than a minute, you are punching your way through the clouds. Soon the blue sky is turning to black. Still the rockets are pushing you ever faster, ever higher. Then they stop. You are in space.

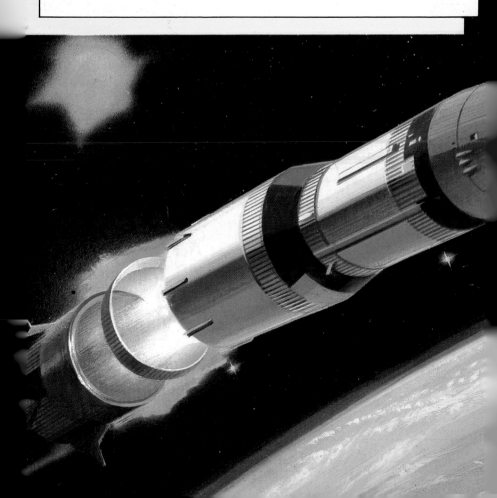

ABOVE THE ATMOSPHERE

Around our planet is a thick layer of air called the atmosphere. In a spacecraft we can climb through the earth's atmosphere into space. In space there is no air, no rain, no snow. It is very hot in the sunlight and very cold in the shade. And everything in space is moving—the earth, the moon, the sun, and the other stars.

Escape from Earth

The earth pulls everything toward it. This pull is called gravity. Rockets beat gravity and get through the earth's atmosphere by traveling very very fast. How fast? About 17,000 miles an hour.

Rockets have to burn several tons of fuel every minute to make them go fast enough to beat gravity. Launch craft have to be very big to carry all this fuel. Some are as tall as office blocks.

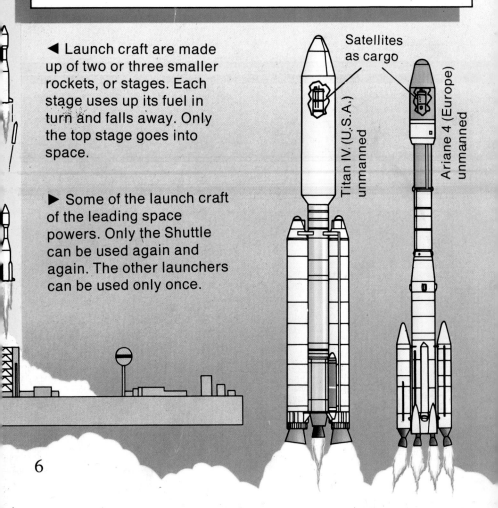

◄ Launch craft are made up of two or three smaller rockets, or stages. Each stage uses up its fuel in turn and falls away. Only the top stage goes into space.

► Some of the launch craft of the leading space powers. Only the Shuttle can be used again and again. The other launchers can be used only once.

Satellites as cargo

Titan IV. (U.S.A.) unmanned

Ariane 4 (Europe) unmanned

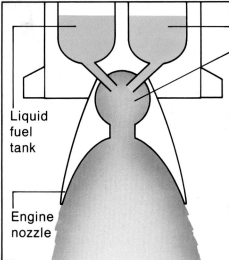

Liquid oxygen tank

Combustion chamber

Liquid fuel tank

Engine nozzle

ROCKET POWER
As well as fuel, rockets carry oxygen to burn the fuel. In a rocket engine, the fuel and oxygen are pumped into a chamber and set on fire. Hot gases are produced which shoot backward out of the engine nozzle. This makes the rocket shoot forward.

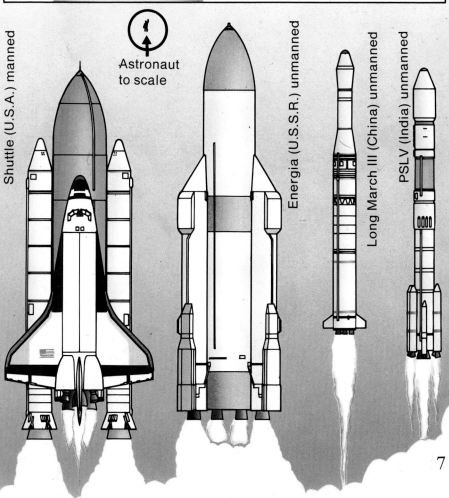

Shuttle (U.S.A.) manned

Astronaut to scale

Energia (U.S.S.R.) unmanned

Long March III (China) unmanned

PSLV (India) unmanned

Satellites in Orbit

When a spacecraft goes into space it starts circling the earth. It travels along the same circular path all the time. We call this path, an orbit.

Some spacecraft leave the earth's orbit to head for other planets, but most stay circling the earth. These are called satellites. We use satellites for all sorts of reasons. Some take pictures of the clouds to help the weather forecasters. Communication satellites carry television and telephone signals. Astronomy satellites look at the stars.

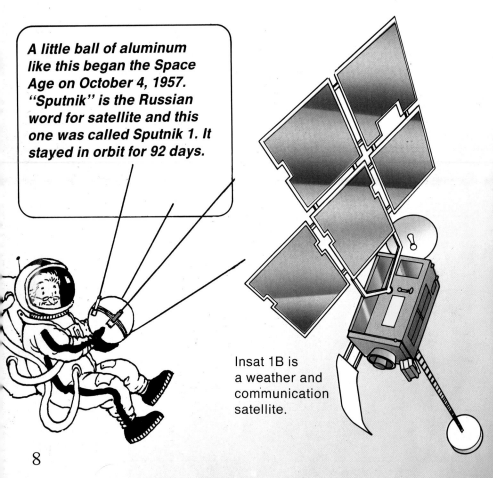

A little ball of aluminum like this began the Space Age on October 4, 1957. "Sputnik" is the Russian word for satellite and this one was called Sputnik 1. It stayed in orbit for 92 days.

Insat 1B is a weather and communication satellite.

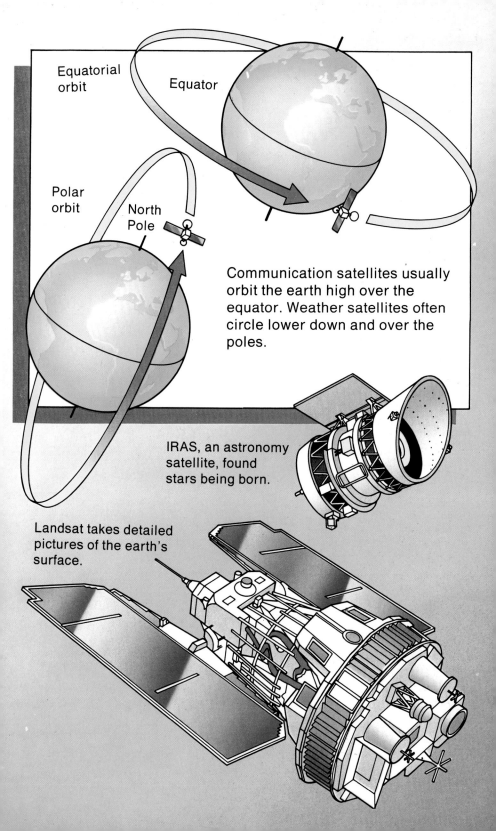

Equatorial orbit

Equator

Polar orbit

North Pole

Communication satellites usually orbit the earth high over the equator. Weather satellites often circle lower down and over the poles.

IRAS, an astronomy satellite, found stars being born.

Landsat takes detailed pictures of the earth's surface.

Space Planes

Ordinary launch craft can be used only once. This is very wasteful, and so a new kind of launcher was designed, a space plane that can be launched again and again. The first space plane was built in the United States. It is called the Shuttle. Now other countries are building space planes, too.

The Shuttle has three main parts—an orbiter, an external fuel tank, and rocket boosters called SRBs. Only the fuel tank cannot be reused.

The orbiter is the main part of the Shuttle. It carries the crew and the cargo, or payload. The first Shuttle flight took place on April 12, 1981. The orbiter was called *Columbia*. The other U.S. orbiters are *Discovery* and *Atlantis*.

Orbiter

Payload bay

NASA

United States

USA

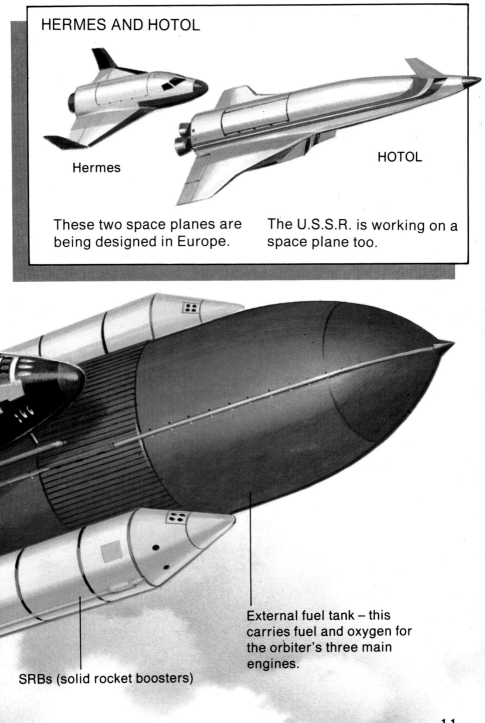

HERMES AND HOTOL

Hermes

HOTOL

These two space planes are being designed in Europe.

The U.S.S.R. is working on a space plane too.

External fuel tank – this carries fuel and oxygen for the orbiter's three main engines.

SRBs (solid rocket boosters)

Shuttle Missions

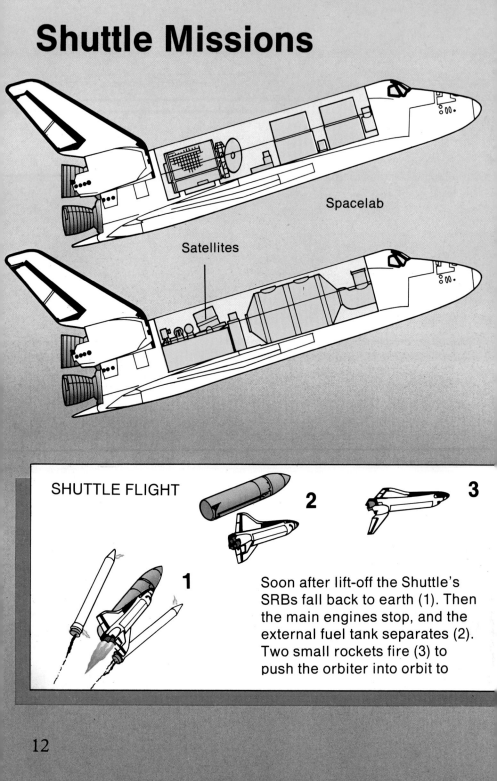

Spacelab

Satellites

SHUTTLE FLIGHT

2

3

1

Soon after lift-off the Shuttle's SRBs fall back to earth (1). Then the main engines stop, and the external fuel tank separates (2). Two small rockets fire (3) to push the orbiter into orbit to

SPACE BALL

If a Shuttle breaks down in space, another will go to the rescue. The crew of the crippled Shuttle will travel to the rescue craft in a rescue ball. The ball has its own air supply, and a small window. There is only room for one person inside, rolled up like a ball to fit in.

One of the main jobs of the Shuttle is to launch satellites. Several satellites can be carried in the orbiter's huge payload bay, which is nearly big enough to hold a railroad car. Sometimes the Shuttle carries a special payload, called Spacelab. This is a space laboratory. Astronaut-scientists are able to carry out all kinds of experiments inside it.

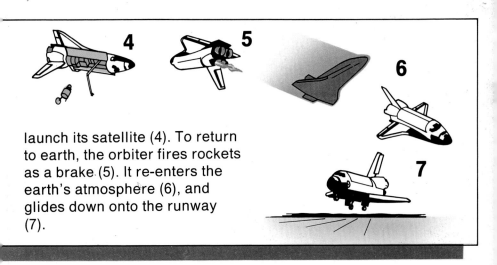

launch its satellite (4). To return to earth, the orbiter fires rockets as a brake (5). It re-enters the earth's atmosphere (6), and glides down onto the runway (7).

Make a Shuttle Glider

You'll need some tracing paper and thin cardboard, a pencil, and some glue, scissors, sticky tape, and paperclips.

Fold the tracing paper in half and place the fold along the bottom edge of the main wing. Trace around the wing. Then, holding the bottom half of the paper where it is, open the top half and trace the wing again. You now have a tracing of the two joined wings. Now trace around the front wing twice and the Shuttle body once. Glue all the tracings on the card and cut them out.

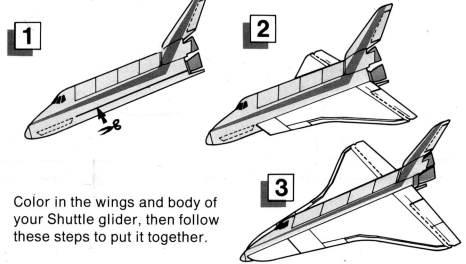

Color in the wings and body of your Shuttle glider, then follow these steps to put it together.

1. Cut along the thick line near the bottom of the glider body. Cut and fold the rudder on its tail.

2. Cut and fold the flaps on the main wing. Now slot the wing into the body. If necessary, use sticky tape to hold it in place.

3. Fold the front wings and glue the flaps onto the body. Now fix a paperclip on the nose and try launching your glider. If it needs more weight, add another paperclip.

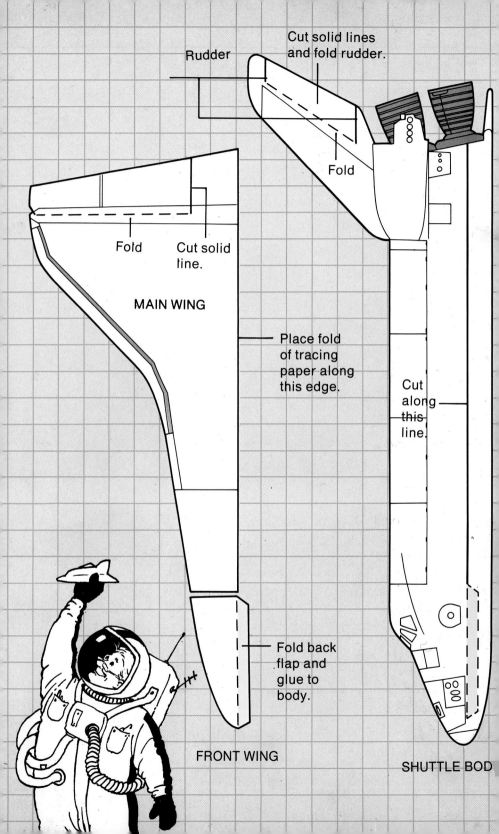

Rudder

Cut solid lines
and fold rudder.

Fold

Fold   Cut solid
          line.

MAIN WING

Place fold
of tracing
paper along
this edge.

Cut
along
this
line.

Fold back
flap and
glue to
body.

FRONT WING

SHUTTLE BOD

Humans in Space

In English we call space travelers astronauts. The Russians call them cosmonauts. Astronauts have to train for many months before they are ready to go into space. They practice everything they will do, and they spend a lot of time training in dummy spacecraft on the ground. The astronauts who will fly the spacecraft train in high-speed jet aircraft.

Would you like to travel in space? Perhaps you would like to work in a space station one day. These are large spacecraft which stay in orbit for a very long time.

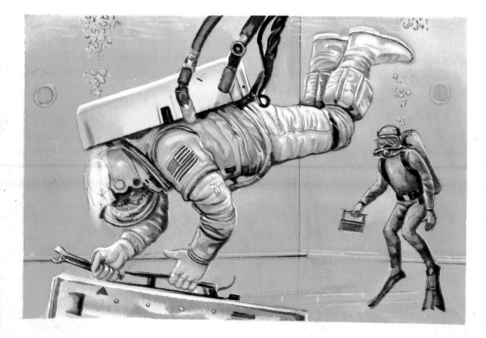

▲ Floating in water is very like floating in space. This is why astronauts practice spacewalking in water tanks.

▶ This is what well-dressed astronauts wear to walk on the moon. The suit protects them and gives them oxygen.

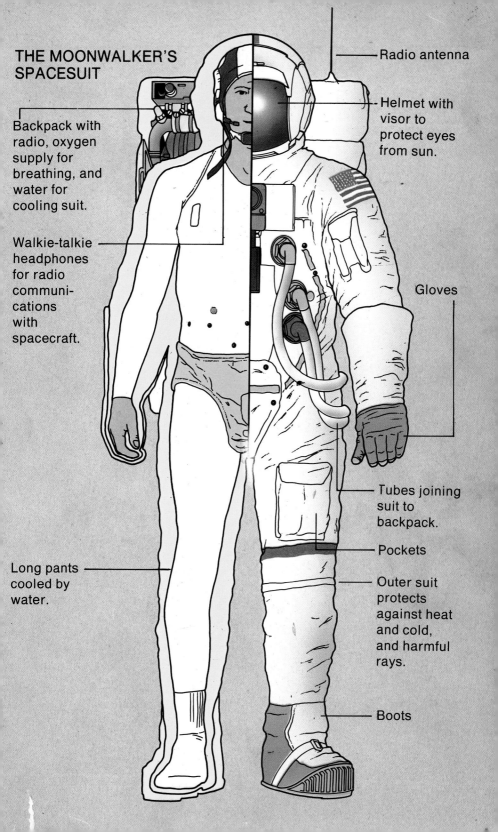

THE MOONWALKER'S SPACESUIT

Radio antenna

Backpack with radio, oxygen supply for breathing, and water for cooling suit.

Helmet with visor to protect eyes from sun.

Walkie-talkie headphones for radio communications with spacecraft.

Gloves

Long pants cooled by water.

Tubes joining suit to backpack.

Pockets

Outer suit protects against heat and cold, and harmful rays.

Boots

Living in Space

What is it like living in space? The first thing astronauts notice is that they have lost weight—all their weight. They are weightless and they just float around in the air. Imagine what it's like. Try turning a somersault. You'll just go around and around and around. Weightlessness affects everything astronauts do in space. It affects the way they eat, sleep, and wash.

Above you can see the Soviet space station Mir. Cosmonauts live and work there for many months at a time, ferrying to and from it in a spacecraft called Soyuz. The solar panels on each side of Mir make electricity from sunlight, to power the station.

▲ You have to be careful when you drink or wash in space. Liquids don't pour when they are weightless, they just float about in tiny drops. To drink, you can squirt it into your mouth or suck through a straw.

▼ You can't walk about in space, as there is nothing to keep your feet down. On earth, gravity holds you on the ground. Because there is no gravity in space, you just float around.

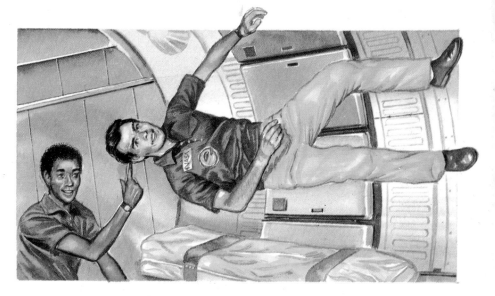

MAKE A SPACE STATION

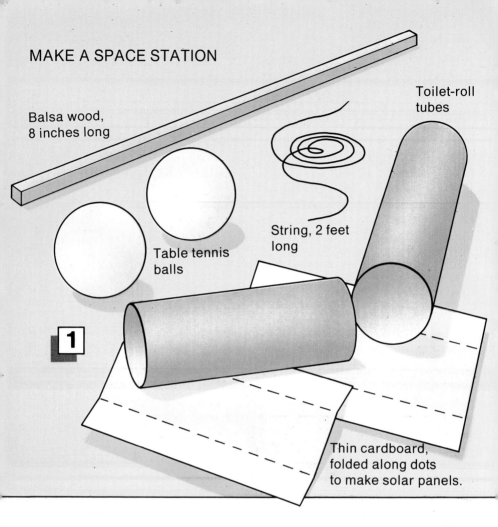

Balsa wood, 8 inches long

Toilet-roll tubes

Table tennis balls

String, 2 feet long

Thin cardboard, folded along dots to make solar panels.

Living in Space—2

There isn't a lot of room for working inside ordinary spacecraft. They can't stay in space for very long, either. Scientists want room to work, and they need to stay in space a long time. That is why space stations are built.

The Soviet space station Mir has been in orbit since 1986, and cosmonauts have stayed in it for nearly a year at a time. In the 1990s, a new international space station will be put into orbit.

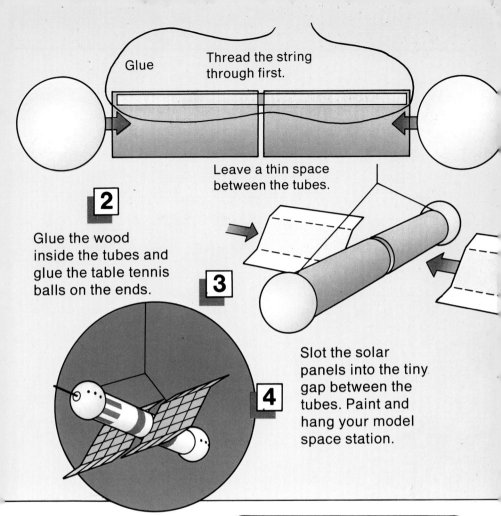

Glue

Thread the string
through first.

Leave a thin space
between the tubes.

2

Glue the wood
inside the tubes and
glue the table tennis
balls on the ends.

3

Slot the solar
panels into the tiny
gap between the
tubes. Paint and
hang your model
space station.

4

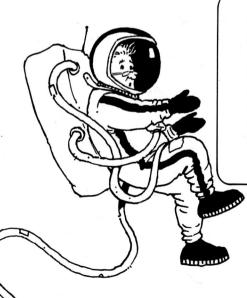

*One of the most exciting
things to do in space is
spacewalking. This is when
astronauts go outside a
spacecraft or station to carry
out experiments or repairs.
Its correct name is EVA,
which stands for extra-
vehicular activity.*

21

Journey to the Moon

In July 1969 the greatest adventure of all time began. American astronauts went to the moon and walked on its surface. Below is the astronauts' landing craft and moon buggy. Lunar means moon, and their landing craft was called a lunar module.

FROM EARTH TO MOON

It took Apollo nearly three days to reach the moon. The astronauts blasted off from earth in a rocket as tall as a skyscraper, and they returned in a capsule smaller than a mini car.

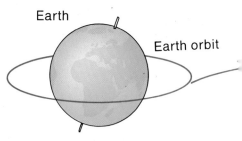

Earth

Earth orbit

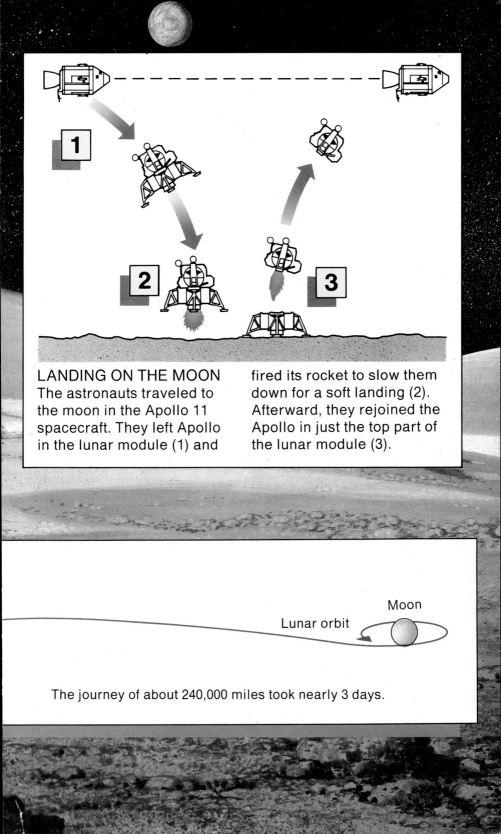

LANDING ON THE MOON

The astronauts traveled to the moon in the Apollo 11 spacecraft. They left Apollo in the lunar module (1) and fired its rocket to slow them down for a soft landing (2). Afterward, they rejoined the Apollo in just the top part of the lunar module (3).

Moon

Lunar orbit

The journey of about 240,000 miles took nearly 3 days.

Robot Explorers

Orbiting satellites stay close to the earth all the time, but other spacecraft go much farther afield. The spacecraft that are called probes visit the planets. They travel for millions of miles to take close-up pictures of the planets and send back all kinds of other information. Space probes have visited Mercury, Venus, Mars, Jupiter, Saturn, Uranus, and Neptune.

Venera probe
(U.S.S.R.)

Some of the Venera probes have landed on the surface of Venus. They found that its temperature is 840°F. If humans weren't roasted alive, they would be crushed to death on Venus—its air pressure is 100 times greater than Earth's.

PRESSURE CRUSHER

Hold out your hand. Did you know that you're holding about 100 pounds? This is the weight of the air, or air pressure. You can't feel it because the air is pressing up on your hand as well. On Venus, humans would crumple like the bottle in the experiment shown here.

This experiment shows how powerful air pressure can be. You'll need a soft plastic bottle with a screw top, like a lemonade bottle, and a pair of gloves to protect your hands.

Ask an adult to fill the bottle with hot water. When the bottle is hot, pour the water out and screw the cap on tightly.

Run cold water over the bottle. It collapses! That's because the steamy air in it cools and shrinks, making the pressure inside much lower than outside.

Robot Explorers—2

Because the planets are so far away from earth, space probes take months or even years to travel to them. Some probes visit more than one planet. The American probe, Voyager 2, has visited four planets—Jupiter, Saturn, Uranus, and Neptune. It is now heading far out into deep space where we will lose contact with it.

In 1976, two American Viking probes landed on Mars. The probes didn't find any Martians though. In fact they didn't find any signs of life at all.

▼ Part of the Viking probe photographed Mars while orbiting it.

▼ The Viking probe's lander took samples of the soil and tested it for signs of life.

SPACE MESSAGES

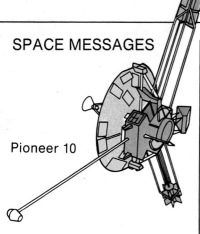

Pioneer 10

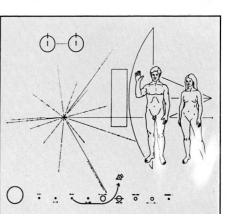

·Pioneer's message

▲ The U.S. space probes, Pioneer 10 and 11, are now heading for the stars. They are carrying a picture to show where they came from and who sent them. One day, another life form may find them and learn about us and our planet.

▶ What kind of message would you send on a space probe? What sort of things would you choose to describe life on earth?

Find a metal box to hold the things you choose for your space message. Metal lasts longer and will give your message more protection.

Mission to Mars

One day humans will travel to other planets. After Venus, Mars is the nearest planet to earth. It is colder than the earth and has little air, but humans could survive there. They will need to live in special shelters and to wear spacesuits when they go outside.

American and Soviet scientists are making plans to visit Mars early next century. It is over 37 million miles away, so they will have to build a very large spacecraft to carry enough fuel and food for the long journey.

Power station

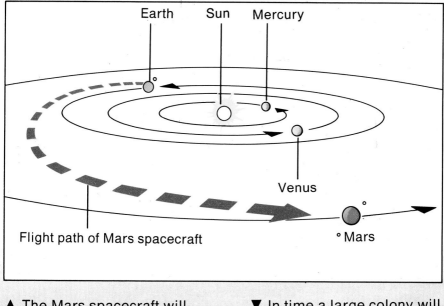

Earth Sun Mercury

Venus

Flight path of Mars spacecraft

° Mars

▲ The Mars spacecraft will take as long as a year to travel to the planet. It will follow a curved path through space.

▼ In time a large colony will grow up on Mars. The people will mine rocks and minerals and grow their own food.

Mars shuttle

Landing pads

Living domes

Glossary

Air pressure
The push of the earth's atmosphere against its surface.

Astronaut
Someone who has trained to travel in space.

Atmosphere
The layer of gases that surrounds a planet. The earth's atmosphere is the air.

Combustion chamber
In a rocket engine, the place where fuel and oxygen are burned.

Cosmonaut
Russian word for astronaut.

EVA
This stands for extra-vehicular activity and means spacewalking.

External fuel tank
The only part of the Shuttle that is not used again. It carries fuel and liquid oxygen for the orbiter's main engines.

Gravity
The invisible force that pulls things toward the earth. Gravity gives things weight.

Launch craft
The craft or vehicle that carries spacecraft into space. It is usually made up of two or three parts or stages.

Liquid oxygen
Because there in no oxygen in space, most rockets carry tanks of liquid oxygen to burn in their engines.

Lunar Orbit
The path of a spacecraft around the moon

Orbit
The path of one body around another. Space satellites orbit the earth.

Orbiter
The main part of the Shuttle, which carries the crew and payload.

Payload
A cargo that is carried into space.

Planet

A body in space that orbits a star. The earth is a planet, as are Venus and Mars. They and the other planets orbit the sun, which is a star.

Probe

A spacecraft that travels deep into space, usually to the planets.

Rocket

The only kind of engine that can work in space. It carries its own oxygen to burn its fuel, unlike ordinary engines.

Satellite

Spacecraft that orbits the earth.

Shuttle

The U.S. space plane. It has three main parts—an orbiter, two SRBs, and an external fuel tank.

Spacecraft

A craft or vehicle that travels into space. Satellites and probes are spacecraft.

Spacelab

A laboratory that is carried inside the Shuttle's payload bay. Astronaut-scientists carry out experiments in it.

Space plane

A launch craft that can be used again and again. The Shuttle is an example of a space plane.

Space station

A large spacecraft that orbits the earth for a very long time.

Spacesuit

Special clothing which protects astronauts when they go on spacewalks.

Spacewalk

Going outside a spacecraft to carry out experiments or repairs. Its correct name is EVA.

SRB

This stands for solid rocket booster. Two SRBs help to launch the Shuttle. They parachute back to earth shortly after lift-off so they can be used again.

Stage

One of the two or three rockets in a launch craft. Each stage uses up its fuel in turn as it gives the stage above a piggyback ride into space.

Index